THE PRACTICAL STRATEGIES SERIES
IN AUTISM EDUCATION

series editors

FRANCES A. KARNES & KRISTEN R. STEPHENS

An Introduction
to Children With Autism

Tammy D. Barry, Ph.D.

Routledge
Taylor & Francis Group

NEW YORK AND LONDON

First published 2009 by Prufrock Press Inc.

Published 2021 by Routledge
605 Third Avenue, New York, NY 10017
2 Park Square, Milton Park, Abingdon, Oxon OX14 4RN

Routledge is an imprint of the Taylor & Francis Group, an informa business

ISBN 13: 978-1-59363-370-7 (pbk)

Contents

Series Preface

The Practical Strategies Series in Autism offers teachers, counselors, administrators, parents, and other interested parties up-to-date information on a variety of issues pertaining to the characteristics, diagnosis, treatment, and education of students with autism spectrum disorders. Each guide addresses a focused topic and is written by an individual with authority on the issue. Several guides have been published. Among the titles are:

- *An Introduction to Children With Autism*
- *Diagnosis and Treatment of Children With Autism Spectrum Disorders*
- *Educational Strategies for Children With Autism Spectrum Disorders*

For a current listing of available guides within the series, please contact Prufrock Press at 800-998-2208 or visit http://www.prufrock.com.

Autism spectrum disorder, or autism, is one of the Pervasive Developmental Disorders (PDDs), a category within the text revision of the fourth edition of the *Diagnostic and Statistical Manual of Mental Health Disorders (DSM-IV-TR)*, that are characterized by severe and pervasive impairment in social interaction and communication, as well as the presence of stereotyped behaviors or restricted activities and circumscribed interests (American Psychiatric Association [APA], 2000). This category of disorders includes Rett's disorder, Childhood Disintegrative Disorder, autism, Asperger's syndrome, and Pervasive Developmental Disorder–Not Otherwise Specified (PDD-NOS). In the current literature, the PDDs often are collectively referred to as autism spectrum disorders or ASDs (Mesibov, Shea, & Schopler, 2004; National Institute of Mental Health, 2008).

The prevalence rates for autism and related disorders have been on the rise. A recent epidemiological review reported rates at approximately 1 per 1,000 children (Fombonne, 2003), whereas the Centers for Disease Control and Prevention currently estimate prevalence rates at 2 to 6 per 1,000 (or from 1 in 500 to 1 in 150 children; National Institute of Mental Health,

2008). Risk for a diagnosis of autism or a related disorder is approximately 4 times greater for boys than girls (APA, 2000).

This category of disorders has been associated with a number of neurological signs and symptoms and sometimes co-occurs with a diverse group of general medical conditions, including chromosomal and central nervous system abnormalities, among others. Approximately 25% of individuals with autism or a related disorder experience seizures, a rate much higher than that of the general population (APA, 2000; Mesibov, Adams, & Klinger, 1997). The significantly higher prevalence rates of these disorders among siblings, as well as the transmission of a broader behavioral phenotype among families, underscore a possible genetic etiology (Mesibov et al., 1997; Pennington, 2002).

Symptoms of Autism and Related Disorders

Symptoms of the three core areas of impairment among individuals with autism and related disorders, as well as concomitant problems within their social environments, are listed in Table 1.

First, individuals with autism demonstrate core impairment in both the quantity and quality of their social interactions (APA, 2000). Symptoms consistent with this impairment include deficits in regulation of social interaction through nonverbal behaviors, such as eye contact, body postures, gestures, and facial expressions. Along with this is a deficit in joint attention; for example, young children with autism do not share attention by looking between an object and caregiver or pointing to objects (Klinger, Dawson, & Renner, 2003). Likewise, individuals with autism are much less likely to spontaneously share their interests with others, including with caregivers (Pennington, 2002). For instance, they often exhibit minimal showing, bringing, and pointing behaviors. They frequently engage in solitary play, have an unusual social style, and fail to develop age-appropriate peer relationships. Young children with autism may have no interest in establishing friendships, whereas older children may have such an interest but lack the skills to do so. When individuals

Table 1
Symptoms and Concomitant Problems

Core Area of Impairment	Symptoms	Example Concomitant Problems
Qualitative impairments in social interaction	• Impairment in the use of nonverbal behaviors (e.g., gaze, facial expression, body postures, and gestures) • Failure to develop age-appropriate peer relationships • Lack of showing, bringing, pointing, or otherwise sharing of enjoyment or interests • Lack of social or emotional reciprocity	• Poor play skills • Problems making friends • Withdrawal from others • Hyperactivity and impulsivity • Aggression and self-injury • Temper tantrums
Qualitative impairments in communication	• Delay in development or lack of spoken language without compensation through alternative modes of communication • Impaired ability to initiate or sustain conversation • Stereotyped and repetitive use of language or idiosyncratic language • Lack of age-appropriate make-believe or social imitative play	• Poor academic performance • Expressive language impairment relative to receptive language • Eating problems • Sleeping problems • Abnormalities in mood or affect • Anxiety/depression
Restricted, repetitive. and stereotyped patterns of behavior, interests, and activities	• Preoccupation with stereotyped and restricted interests (intensity of focus) • Inflexible adherence to routines or rituals that are nonfunctional • Stereotypical and repetitive motor mannerisms (e.g., finger flapping or twisting) or complex body movements • Preoccupation with parts of objects	• Problems with conversations (e.g., only wants to talk about area of interest; changes subject to restricted interest) • Inability to adapt to changes (e.g., freezes or tantrums when routine changes) • Withdrawal into repetitive movement

(APA, 2000)

with autism engage in social interaction, there typically is a lack of reciprocity (Volkmar & Lord, 2007). For example, they often do not understand give-and-take in social games and frequently have no response or an inappropriate response to others' emotions, including distress (APA, 2000). Some individuals with autism display an aversion to physical contact, whereas others may inappropriately invade others' physical boundaries during social interactions.

Individuals with autism typically show difficulties with social imitation, including problems replicating the movements of others or an awkward imitation style (Klinger et al., 2003). Recent research suggests that this may be due to fewer mirror neurons, which are those involved in learning by watching and observing others. This appears to be due to an increased amount of improperly functioning gray matter in specific brain regions linked to the mirror neuron system (e.g., parietal lobe; Ashtari et al., 2007).

A second core impairment for individuals with autism is in the area of language development and the qualitative nature of their communication (APA, 2000). Individuals with autism have delayed language development with a lack of compensation with nonverbal behaviors, such as gesturing or miming. For approximately 35% to 40% of those individuals diagnosed, functional language never develops (Mesibov et al., 1997). If language does develop, the individual with autism may show stereotyped, repetitive, and idiosyncratic language, including echolalia (repetition of what is heard), jargon, and pronoun reversal (Volkmar & Lord, 2007). Abnormalities in speech, such as the pitch, rate, or prosody (rhythm, stress, and intonation) of the speech, often are noted (APA, 2000). Individuals with autism also have difficulty initiating and sustaining conversation with others. They may engage in long, elaborate monologues or have difficulty answering others' questions, again lacking the give-and-take reciprocity that is natural in communication with others. Finally, individuals with autism demonstrate play skills that typically are below their expected developmental level, often showing impairments in pretend play, symbolic play, and social imitative play (APA, 2000; Pennington, 2002).

The third core problem area for individuals with autism is their restricted, repetitive, and stereotyped behaviors or circumscribed interests (APA, 2000). For instance, individuals with autism often exhibit a preoccupation with a particular activity or topic that is unusual in intensity or focus. Likewise, individuals with autism habitually and inflexibly adhere to specific routines or rituals that may serve no function (Volkmar & Lord, 2007). Examples include lining up toys, insisting on the same route to school, or engaging in complex verbal rituals. They may exhibit intense distress when a routine is changed, even trivially. In addition, individuals with autism often exhibit stereotyped and repetitive motor mannerisms and posturing, such as hand flapping, finger flicking, rocking, walking on toes, or even complex whole body movements (Pennington, 2002). Finally, a persistent preoccupation with parts of objects (e.g., spinning wheels on toy cars, door hinges) or an insignificant inanimate object (e.g., piece of string) is a characteristic symptom of autism (APA, 2000).

Individuals with a diagnosis of autism demonstrate a significant level of impairment across all three core areas (i.e., social, language/communication, and restricted, repetitive, and stereotyped behaviors or interests), with an onset of problems in social interaction, language, and play skills prior to the age of 3 years (APA, 2000). The other PDDs are differentiated from autism in the nature of the symptoms' presentation. Individuals with Asperger's syndrome (APA, 2000) exhibit significantly impairing deficits in social interaction, as well as restricted, repetitive, and stereotyped behaviors and interests. However, unlike individuals with autism, those with Asperger's syndrome have no significant language delays. These individuals use single words by age 2 and phrases by age 3. Individuals with Asperger's syndrome also have average to above-average intelligence (no significant cognitive delays) and, other than social interaction, they develop age-appropriate self-help skills and adaptive behavior. Thus, a comorbid or coexisting diagnosis of mental retardation is ruled out for Asperger's syndrome. Individuals with Rett's disorder (APA, 2000) are marked by a deceleration of head growth following normal development, loss of acquired hand skills and poor coordination, loss of social engagement, and severe language impairments. Individuals with Childhood Disintegrative Disorder (APA, 2000) have an apparently normal development for at least the first 2 years after birth, followed by a loss of acquired skills before age 10 in areas such as language, social skills, adaptive behavior, play skills, and motor development. After this loss of skills, the overall impairment profile of an individual with Childhood Disintegrative Disorder is similar to that of individuals with autism (Klinger et al., 2003). Finally, individuals with PDD-NOS (APA, 2000) do not exhibit the necessary symptoms for another PDD diagnosis but, nevertheless, are characterized by communication impairments, social deficits, and/or stereotyped behavior or restricted activities or interests. These impairments are severe and pervasive enough to warrant a diagnosis. Each of the PDD diagnoses is mutually exclusive. That is, an individual would not be diagnosed with more than one of these disorders concurrently.

The Autism Spectrum

There is much heterogeneity within the autism spectrum, with symptoms ranging from mild to quite severe. Individuals with "classic" autism are low functioning; in fact, as many as 75% of individuals with autism have a comorbid diagnosis of mental retardation (APA, 2000), with more recent estimates at less than 70% (Klinger et al., 2003). However, it follows that a proportion of individuals with autism are high functioning, with average to above-average intelligence. Those individuals diagnosed with Asperger's syndrome, by definition, have intellectual abilities also within the average to above-average range. Thus, it often is difficult to differentiate Asperger's syndrome from high functioning autism (HFA). Again, a history of language delay rules out Asperger's syndrome and often helps to make this differential diagnosis (APA, 2000).

Although ASDs are a diagnostic category, it also is important to recognize that individuals with an ASD have their own culture (i.e., shared patterns of human thinking and behavior; Mesibov et al., 2004). In fact, as described by Mesibov and colleagues (2004), teachers, parents, and other family members of a person with an ASD often have to be a "cross-cultural interpreter" by helping to translate expectations of the world around him or her (p. 19). That is, they must help increase the individual's knowledge and skills and make the environment more comprehensible for the individual with an ASD (Mesibov et al., 2004), with the ultimate goals of capitalizing on strengths and ameliorating weaknesses.

As noted earlier, individuals with an ASD are a heterogeneous group, and not any one symptom of ASDs captures all individuals with a diagnosis. Furthermore, there are some fundamental features that often are associated with these disorders but that are not specifically diagnostic criteria. Consideration of these characteristics can aid in better understanding the dissimilarities in how children with an ASD perceive and relate to the world around them and also are an important source of heterogeneity observed within ASDs. The following sections offer a review of these characteristics, as well as case examples of individuals with an ASD exhibiting these characteristics.

Characteristics of Autism

Language

Approximately one in three children with an ASD will not develop functional and communicative language, and those who do develop language demonstrate a pattern of specific deficits. First, verbal individuals with an ASD show deficits in semantic language (i.e., the meaning of communication). For example, persons with an ASD often exhibit pronoun reversals (referring to themselves as "you" and others as "I") that may be compensated for by diminished pronoun use (i.e., using names instead of pronouns) as they get older (Mesibov et al., 1997). Echolalia, which is meaningless verbatim repetition of previously heard language, is quite common among individuals with an ASD and may either be immediate echolalia (repeating words or phrases just heard) or delayed echolalia (repeating something heard hours or even days earlier). Often, delayed echolalia involves repeating phrases heard in a commercial, television program, or movie. Echolalia once was viewed as a self-stimulatory behavior but is more likely an attempt to communicate and could be a precursor to more advanced language (Mesibov et al., 1997). Nevertheless, it is inflexible and often incompatible with the situation and is, therefore, limited in its usefulness.

The lack of understanding of the semantic content of language experienced by people with an ASD often translates into difficulty perceiving meaning and drawing relationships between ideas and events (Mesibov et al., 2004). For example, these individuals may not respond appropriately to requests not because of stubbornness or defiance but because they do not understand the verbal demand. This may be the case for even the highest functioning individuals with an ASD. Semantic difficulties also are noticed at the single word level. For instance, because of their difficulties in understanding or generalizing meaning, children with an ASD tend to use a limited range of words in conversation even if they have a fully developed vocabulary (Mesibov et al., 1997). Indeed, their receptive language, or comprehension, often is below that of their expressive language, particularly in high-functioning individuals with an ASD (APA, 2000). They often have difficulty understanding abstract words, such as adverbs and adjectives, relative to their understanding of words describing more concrete, tangible objects, such as nouns. This language difficulty may exacerbate some of their problems in social interactions, such as their difficulties recognizing and labeling their own and others' emotions. Because of these problems with abstract language, individuals with an ASD often misunderstand idioms or slang language, typically interpreting such phrases in a concrete and literal way.

Second, verbal individuals with an ASD demonstrate deficits with the pragmatic aspects of language, or the use of language in social contexts (Mesibov et al., 1997). For example, they may focus on irrelevant details during a conversation. These details may not only be irrelevant but also socially bizarre (e.g., describing all of the highways taken and the number of miles per highway to take a trip). Individuals with an ASD may provide too much information, wrongly assuming that the listener has no prior knowledge, or may launch into a topic area without appropriate explanation, inappropriately assuming that the listener has significant prior knowledge of the subject matter.

Difficulties with the pragmatics of language have been linked to the tendency for individuals with an ASD to perseverate on one topic area in conversation, which is a cardinal characteristic of ASDs. Usually this preferred conversation topic focuses on their idiosyncratic interests. The selected topic area may be socially acceptable (e.g., sports) but nevertheless odd in the degree to which the individual pursues the topic and dominates the conversation. At other times, the topic may be socially unusual (e.g., a detailed discussion of train schedules). Connected with their single-minded pursuit of conversing exclusively about their own topic of interest, individuals with an ASD often interrupt and inappropriately shift conversations back to their interest area. They have extreme difficulty with turn-taking in conversation and with staying on topic, especially when the conversation is shifted by someone else and particularly if the new topic is not one of perceived relevance to them. In addition, they exhibit a lower than typical frequency of social repairs when there is a communication breakdown during a conversation with another person (Mesibov et al., 1997).

Not only are individuals with an ASD likely to interrupt conversations, but they also may respond to others' questions or probes with complete silence, failing to realize that they should respond (Mesibov et al., 1997). Many of the nonverbal deficits affiliated with ASDs stem from a problem grasping pragmatic language skills. For example, they often do not notice or respond to nonverbal cues, such as changes in others' body language or mood during conversation, or they may not engage in appropriate eye contact. They may monopolize conversations well beyond the other person's level of interest or they may walk away when others are attempting to interact with them (Baron-Cohen & Bolton, 1993). In short, individuals with an ASD do not seem to implicitly learn the rules of social conversation (Tager-Flusberg, 1993). It is notable, however, that despite this significant pattern of deficits in the semantic and pragmatic aspects of language, individuals with an ASD are not specifically impaired in speech (pronunciation, articulation) and appear to be able to learn language structure, grammatical rules, and appropriate word order (Mesibov et al., 1997).

Case Example

Steven, a 12-year-old boy with Asperger's syndrome, was preoccupied with Pokémon. He played the videogames virtually nonstop when he was at home, to the exclusion of engaging in meaningful interactions with his siblings or mother. He collected Pokémon trading cards, and he repeatedly got discipline referrals at school for playing with the cards or talking to his classmates about the cards during classroom instruction time. Steven conversed incessantly about Pokémon with everyone he met, assuming that others' interest in and knowledge of the subject was at his level. Steven also made up elaborate stories about the Pokémon characters and spoke repeatedly about his plans to get a job developing new Pokémon videogames after graduation from high school. When others tried to change the topic of conversation, Steven would interrupt them or talk over them to bring the topic back to Pokémon. He ignored subtle nonverbal cues of disinterest from others during such conversations, and he was quite perplexed if anyone explicitly stated their disinterest in Pokémon, typically continuing his monologue on the subject.

Cognitive

No single cognitive deficit has been identified as occurring in all individuals with an ASD and those cognitive deficits that have been identified are not specific only to ASDs, often occurring in other disorders as well (Klinger & Renner, 2000). Nevertheless, there are clusters of cognitive differences that aid in understanding the characteristics of the ASDs and that may shed some light on possible etiological factors. Interestingly, for each of these cognitive domains, individuals with ASDs tend to show a pattern of both intact and impaired abilities.

One such cognitive domain is executive functioning, which involves planning and problem solving to achieve a goal. Impulse control, inhibition, and working memory are important precursors of executive function (Klinger & Renner, 2000). Whereas the ability to inhibit a proponent response and to maintain a cognitive set is intact in individuals with an ASD, they exhibit impairments in their ability to plan a future response, respond flexibly to their environment, shift cognitive sets, and organize themselves or their surroundings (e.g., Hill, 2008; McEvoy, Rogers, & Pennington, 1993; Ozonoff & Jensen, 1999). This is particularly true of older or higher functioning individuals (Klinger & Renner, 2000). Individuals with an ASD often show a propensity for routines and can be quite perseverative (Mesibov et al., 1997). They exhibit impairments in organizing and sequencing (Mesibov et al., 2004), including difficulty integrating several elements to achieve a goal. They seem to have particular difficulty with simultaneously focusing attention on both the situation at hand and a later outcome. Individuals with an ASD also have difficulties with tasks that place demands on working memory (i.e., mentally storing and manipulating information in short-term memory). They may become very confused during a sequence of steps and will stop and restart repeatedly, or perhaps perform the steps in an irrational order (Mesibov et al., 2004).

Individuals with an ASD also often show impairments in theory of mind, which is the ability to attribute mental states, such as beliefs, desires, and intentions, to oneself and others (Klinger & Renner, 2000). Because of their difficulties taking another person's perspective that is different from their own, individuals with an ASD do not readily understand how another person can be deceived or hold a false belief. In a classic test of theory of mind, a puppet is shown a toy in a certain location, then the puppet is removed from the scene and the toy is moved to a new location, and the puppet then returns to the scene. When asked, most children with an ASD will report that the puppet will search for the toy in the new location (Mesibov et al., 1997). Even when they can describe the other's visual perspective (i.e., they state that the puppet indeed did not see the toy being moved), they still may not understand that another's belief or knowledge could differ from their own (i.e., that the puppet does not know the toy is in the new location because the puppet did not see it moved; Mesibov et al., 1997). Most research suggests that theory of mind may be delayed in development, rather than entirely absent, in individuals with an ASD (Klinger & Renner, 2000).

Weak central coherence, or an inability to understand context because of a preference for processing parts of a stimulus rather than the whole stimulus, has been documented among individuals with an ASD (Frith, 2000; Happé, 1999). That is, they tend to "focus on details rather than gestalts" (Mesibov et al., 1997, p. 72). For example, children with an ASD are able to complete puzzles that are turned over so that the picture cannot be seen as easily as if the picture were in view. They do not benefit from seeing the whole picture because they are focused on the puzzle parts. Indeed, although individuals with an ASD have an intact ability to process information at an analytical level, research suggests that they have difficulty with global level processing. For instance, persons with an ASD may have problems automatically abstracting information and integrating it across experiences and settings (Klinger & Renner, 2000). This may explain why some higher functioning individuals with an ASD can be quite adept at difficult subject matter (e.g., engineering) but have extreme difficulty expressing themselves through language and live in virtual social isolation. They seem to have difficulty encoding new information into memory (Mesibov et al., 1997). That is, whereas typically developing individuals will abstract across different examples to form a prototype (a summary representation) of a new category for their memory schemata, those individuals with an ASD have difficulty forming a prototype due to their impairments in abstraction (Klinger et al., 2003). Thus, categorization requiring reliance on a prototype (without any defining rules) is impaired in children with an ASD, whereas their categorization skills are intact when given a rule that defines category membership (Mesibov et al., 1997). In short, individuals with an ASD appear impaired in their implicit (automatic) learning skills (Klinger et al., 2003).

Although children with an ASD appear to have intact abilities to search and filter through information, as well as select and sustain their attention, they exhibit difficulties orienting (i.e., disengaging and shifting) their attention (Courchesne et al., 1994; Klinger & Renner, 2000). In fact, some caregivers and teachers initially suspect that a child later diagnosed with an ASD is deaf (Mesibov et al., 1997), because the child seems to be so disconnected and nonresponsive to introduced environmental stimuli. Individuals with an ASD exhibit selective attention (attending to salient stimuli), including attention to details. However, they often focus on narrow, irrelevant aspects of their environment. Mesibov and colleagues (2004) captured this by describing how "they might enter a room and comment on the sounds of the fan, while ignoring the lighted birthday cake on the table" (p. 21). This can explain impairment in communication with others as well. For example, during a conversation with another person, a child with ASD may focus on the person's shirt buttons or hairline, rather than on his or her facial expressions. These individuals' intact sustained attention, combined with their impaired ability to disengage and shift attention, contributes to their focus on irrelevant or restricted/circumscribed stimuli or topics (Mesibov et al., 1997).

Taken together, this pattern of cognitive deficits may further hinder the social interactions of persons with an ASD. For example, executive dysfunction may interfere with their ability to access stored information or regulate behavior, and deficits in attention orientation may keep them overfocused on stimuli irrelevant to social context (Klinger et al., 2003). Similarly, difficulties with prototype formation may explain some of their impairments with processing social information, which tends to not be rule-governed (Mesibov et al., 1997) and is implicitly learned (Klinger et al., 2003). Individuals with an ASD also have difficulty with generalization (e.g., cannot apply skills from one situation to the next; learn a rule and do not realize that it applies to other situations; Mesibov et al., 2004).

Given the uneven pattern of cognitive functioning, it would be incorrect to only focus on the deficits associated with an ASD. Often, persons with ASD exhibit cognitive strengths that are not only personal strong points but also areas in which they have superior performance compared to their typically developing peers. Indeed, individuals with an ASD demonstrate "peaks and valleys" in their ability to understand information (Mesibov et al., 1997, p. 65). It has been documented that individuals with an ASD perform better on nonverbal, visual-spatial tasks than they do on verbal tasks (Happé, 1999; Mesibov et al., 1997). This difference is demonstrated in a greater nonverbal than verbal IQ score in about 15% to 33% of individuals with an ASD (Flanagan & Kaufman, 2004). However, notably, most individuals with an ASD show no measurable discrepancy between verbal and non-verbal IQ scores. Because of their strong visual memory skills, individuals with autism typically notice even the smallest change in their surroundings (Mesibov et al., 1997). Individuals with an ASD often demonstrate impressive rote memory skills; for example, they may be able to recite train timetables, chemical formulas, or the exact wording of song lyrics (APA, 2000). They also may exhibit savant skills (e.g., in math abilities).

Case Example

Christian, a 9-year-old boy referred for an evaluation for autism, was given an individually administered standardized test of intelligence. He demonstrated an uneven pattern of results on the cognitive evaluation, consistently performing better on nonverbal, visual-spatial tasks when compared to tasks measuring verbal expression, comprehension, or working memory. Notably, Christian demonstrated marked variations in his abilities, scoring at the 99th percentile on a task that required him to recreate a visual design from blocks (where perceiving component parts, rather than the whole object, could be an advantage) but scoring at the first percentile on a task that required him to verbally comprehend and respond to questions requiring judgment about social situations.

Behavioral

Individuals with an ASD sometimes exhibit a pattern of significant externalizing behavioral problems that are associated with, but not fully explained by, their diagnostic symptoms. Such externalizing behaviors include symptoms associated with ADHD, such as hyperactivity, impulsivity, and inattention (APA, 2000; Mesibov et al., 1997), including the problems with prioritizing the importance of details and shifting attention as described earlier. Individuals with an ASD also are highly distractible, particularly by visual stimulation (Mesibov et al., 2004). Sometimes they are distracted by internal cognitions (e.g., compulsions or reviewing memorized facts) or by internal states (e.g., desires). Individuals often feel bombarded by stimulation, with some individuals rapidly exploring and shifting quickly among all stimuli and others shutting out the overwhelming stimuli and narrowly focusing (Mesibov et al., 2004).

Other externalizing behaviors sometimes exhibited by individuals with an ASD include defiance and aggression (Mesibov et al., 1997). Such behaviors may range from being overly resistant, uncooperative, and noncompliant to displaying violent and severe tantrums that include hitting, kicking, biting, and scratching both themselves and others, as well as throwing objects and breaking things (Dominick, Davis, Lainhart, Tager-Flusberg, & Folstein, 2007). These more violent behaviors may escalate into self-aggression. Such externalizing behaviors, although not a diagnostic symptom of an ASD, may stem from these symptoms (e.g., an inability to communicate; Mesibov et al., 2004).

Case Example

Janice, a 9-year-old girl with autism and an estimated full scale IQ of 50, had no functional language. Janice's mother sought treatment services for Janice at an outpatient ASD clinic due to severe temper tantrums, aggression, and self-injurious behavior. When Janice became frustrated, she would hit, kick, and scratch her parents and siblings, and she sometimes threw objects at others. During her most severe tantrums, she would wail and rock uncontrollably. In a recent tantrum in the backseat of the car, Janice hurt the side of her head from beating it against the car door. During the course of treatment, it was clear that Janice was most likely to engage in these behaviors when she was unable to understand demands being placed on her or when she was unable to communicate with others. A more structured environment and schedule system was used to communicate expectations to Janice and a picture communication system was adopted that allowed Janice to more easily convey her basic needs to others. Her aggressive and tantrum behaviors diminished considerably.

Movement

As noted in the review of the third core area of impairment, individuals with an ASD often exhibit stereotyped or repetitive motor mannerisms and posturing that do not serve a specific function (APA, 2000). These motor movements may include odd behaviors such as finger flicking, rocking, or complex whole-body movements. Sometimes the motor movements displayed are age-inappropriate, such as an older child exhibiting hand flapping or toe walking (Pennington, 2002). A consideration of movement disturbances among children with an ASD is important given the fact that movement is an "infant's first language" (Teitelbaum et al., 2004, p. 11909). Indeed, movement disorders have been documented in children who were later diagnosed with autism through a review of videotapes of the children as young as 4 months old. Movement disturbances coded in these videotapes varied from the children exhibiting problems with moving their mouth to delays or qualitative impairments in motor milestones, such as sitting, crawling, and walking, among others (Teitelbaum, Teitelbaum, Nye, Fryman,

& Maurer, 1998). In addition, abnormalities in infant reflexes have been documented in children with an ASD, including a failure to exhibit certain reflexes at the appropriate age or, alternatively, persistent display of an infant reflex well past the age at which it should have been inhibited (Teitelbaum et al., 2004). Some studies have documented early motor movement abnormalities both in lower functioning children with autism and in higher functioning children diagnosed with Asperger's syndrome (e.g., Teitelbaum et al., 2004). In contrast, recent research suggests that both children with autism and children with developmental delays display motor delays relative to typically developing children but only children diagnosed with developmental delays exhibit higher rates of motor abnormalities (Ozonoff et al., 2008). Others have found that children with an ASD and those children with a developmental delay show more repetitive motor mannerisms than typically developing children from around the age of 1 but that the two groups do not differ from one another (Osterling, Dawson, & Munson, 2002). Thus, the research in this area, particularly the specificity of these problems to very young children with an ASD, is somewhat inconclusive. Nevertheless, certainly by the age of 2, repetitive motor mannerisms and stereotypies (mechanical repetitions of the same movement) are hallmark symptoms of an ASD (APA, 2000; Lord, 1995).

Case Example

Austin, a 4-year-old boy with autism, exhibits several abnormal motor movements, including odd postures and stereotypies. For example, when he becomes upset, he extends his head and arches his back in a stiff posture. He often engages in hand-flapping, sometimes in a vertical motion and, at other times, pushes and pulls his arms while they are parallel to the floor. When sitting, he typically rocks back and forth or sways side-to-side. His mouth often is open for minutes at a time, and he engages in some tongue protrusion. Austin also exhibits complex finger rotations and finger flicking.

Affect/Mood

Individuals with an ASD often display abnormalities of mood or affect (APA, 2000). For example, they may demonstrate an emotional response that is apparently inappropriate or out of place for the context or a strong emotional response (e.g., weeping) that does not appear to have an environmental precursor. They also may show unusual blends of different emotions (Klinger et al., 2003). Likewise, their affect may be flat or blunted, lacking in nonverbal enhancements (Mesibov et al., 1997). They also have more difficulty producing affective expressions when requested to show specific emotions (Klinger et al., 2003).

Although high-functioning individuals with an ASD display impairments in social skills, they appear to have a desire for social involvement with others but usually cannot articulate what it means to be someone's friend (Mesibov et al., 1997). They recognize when such social support is lacking and may experience perceptions of poor social support and loneliness (Barnhill, 2001; Bauminger & Kasari, 2000). Even when children with an ASD report having a best friend, the quality of the friendship typically is lacking in several pivotal categories (i.e., companionship, security, and help) relative to typically developing peers (Bauminger & Kasari, 2000), potentially further perpetuating their feelings of loneliness. Further complicating these feelings, children with an ASD are prone to attribute social failures to a lack in their own abilities (Barnhill, 2001). Such feelings of poor social support, increased loneliness and isolation, and negative social attributions that frequently are experienced by individuals with an ASD may be one pathway to the onset of later depression. Indeed, higher functioning adolescents and adults with an ASD are more prone to develop depressive symptoms as they recognize their differences from their peers (APA, 2000; Barnhill, 2001; Mesibov et al., 1997). Depression is a common comorbidity among the ASDs and is associated in a worsening of symptoms, including social withdrawal (Klinger et al., 2003).

Case Example

Bobby, a 16-year-old high-functioning adolescent with autism, presented a need for therapy due to high rates of depressive symptoms. He was included in regular education classrooms in high school, performed average to above average in his schoolwork, and was on track to graduate from high school. Bobby was aware of his diagnosis and his differences from other teenagers at his school. Although he desired to form friendships and to even have a girlfriend, he had no friends. Although a few classmates teased Bobby, he mostly was neglected and ignored by others. Bobby even had difficulty getting along with his younger sister who struggled with her brother's diagnosis. Bobby spent most of his free time engaging with his mother and father, including helping his father with work for his self-owned small business. His mother was aware of Bobby's depression and often was overinvolved in trying to minimize or control his symptoms, which actually seemed to exacerbate his depression. For example, he reported feeling guilty for making his mother cry when he was unable to do some of the things others his age could (e.g., get a part-time job). Bobby experienced many automatic negative thoughts about himself and frequently failed to attempt activities that he was able to do because he felt like he generally was a "failure."

Temperament

Some individuals with an ASD demonstrate high fearfulness, often to common objects, whereas others may exhibit low fearfulness, even in dangerous situations (APA, 2000). Anxiety disorders, including generalized anxiety disorder, obsessive-compulsive disorder, agoraphobia, specific phobias, and separation anxiety disorder, are more prevalent among individuals with an ASD than the general population (Klinger et al., 2003). Individuals with an ASD often show greater variability in their temperament and more problems with self-regulation, even to mildly frustrating events (Konstantareas & Stewart, 2006). Finally, higher functioning individuals with an ASD often display more negative affectivity or mood (Konstantareas & Stewart, 2006).

Case Example

Cameron, an 8-year-old boy with autism, is overly anxious. He repeatedly wrings his hands and bites and picks at his fingernails. When completing schoolwork and other tasks, he must finalize every detail of a task before moving on to the next one. A slow and meticulous worker, this causes some problems when he is working on timed tasks (e.g., he will not quit a task even after time has elapsed). Cameron experiences many symptoms of general anxiety. For example, he is concerned that he will not pass the third grade, despite the fact that he is earning all passing grades. He worries about being tardy and has an obsessive routine in the morning that involves having his parents bring him to school 30 minutes before the school day begins. He also worries about where his mother is when he is at school and who would call her if he were to get sick. At home, Cameron limits himself exclusively to indoor activities because he is afraid of insects and the neighborhood dogs. He has an obsessive routine for toileting that sometimes requires as long as 45 minutes for one toileting incident. Cameron also has trouble sleeping at night because his mind "races with worrying thoughts."

Sleeping and Eating

Children with an ASD often exhibit basic disturbances in sleeping and eating. Individuals with an ASD require less sleep than other members of their family (Klinger et al., 2003). Notably, based on both parent-report and self-report, children with an ASD exhibit more prevalent sleep disturbance than do their typically developing peers (Couturier et al., 2005; Hoffman, Sweeney, Gilliam, & Lopez-Wagner, 2006; Paavonen et al., 2008). The sleep disturbances associated with an ASD involve problems with both sleep quantity and quality, including onset and maintenance of sleep. In fact, rates of sleep problems among this group are estimated as high as 44% to 83% (Richdale, 1999). Although sleep problems are higher among developmental disorders in general (Piazza, Fisher, & Kahng, 1996), the sleep disturbance among individuals with an ASD does not appear to be due to comorbid mental retardation, given that higher rates of these problems are found within individuals with an ASD compared to IQ-matched control groups (Couturier et al., 2005; Paavonen et al., 2008; Richdale & Prior, 1995). Yet, reduced sleep quantity and poorer sleep quality in individuals with an ASD does appear to be associated with the severity of ASD symptoms, including overall scores on global measures of autistic symptoms (e.g., Malow et al., 2006; Schreck, Mulick, & Smith, 2004). Whereas both the quantity of sleep required and the level of sleep disturbances noted among typically developing children decreases with age, this same trend is not found among individuals with an ASD (Schreck & Mulick, 2000), suggesting that sleep problems among this group follow a different developmental trajectory. In addition to onset and maintenance difficulties, some of the problems associated with sleeping include recurrent waking in the night with rocking (APA, 2000), as well as sleep-related fears, daytime sleeping, and negative attitudes toward sleeping (Paavonen et al., 2008).

In addition to sleep problems, individuals with an ASD exhibit significant disturbances in their eating behaviors compared to typically developing peers. According to Schreck, Williams, and Smith (2004), a diagnosis of an ASD is associated with a restriction in food categories and textures, a need for a specific food presentation (e.g., certain plate or utensils; certain way the food is cut or arranged), and greater food refusal overall. Children with an ASD eat fewer foods from each major food group, despite the fact that families of children with and without an ASD do not differ in the amount of foods from each group that they eat. Often adults with an ASD require supervision to ensure they eat a balanced diet (Klinger et al., 2003). Finally, individuals with an ASD also are more likely than the general population to engage in pica, which involves eating nonfood objects (e.g., paint, string, or cloth; APA, 2000).

Case Example

Martin, a 15 year-old high-functioning adolescent boy with autism, demonstrated marked impairment in his sleeping and eating patterns. Martin had difficulty initiating and maintaining sleep at night, often staying up hours past his bedtime, despite the fact that he had inadequate sleep the night before. Martin would only eat his meals from white, ceramic plates, refusing to eat from paper plates or from the colored trays used to serve food in his school cafeteria. Martin required that his meal be arranged on his plate with ample space between foods, and he would not eat a food if it touched another, either during the initial presentation or during the course of eating his meal. Martin preferred only starchy or cheesy foods. For example, when allowed to select his meal at a self-service food bar, Martin chose macaroni and cheese, cheese pizza, spaghetti noodles with no sauce, mashed potatoes, and a buttered roll. He consistently refused to eat any fruits or meats, and limited his vegetables to mainly corn and potatoes. His parents were concerned about his nutritional intake and sleeping patterns, particularly given that Martin was considerably overweight for his height.

Sensory

Individuals with an ASD often show odd or extreme responses to sensory stimuli. Many times, this is manifested as a hypersensitivity to sound, light, or touch (Mesibov et al., 1997). That is, even though individuals with an ASD exhibit inattentiveness in many situations, they may show overattentiveness to certain environmental stimuli (Mesibov et al., 1997, p. 71). For example, they may be distracted by the humming of fluorescent lights, may pick up barely visible pieces of lint, or may cover their ears when others are talking at a normal tone.

Individuals with an ASD sometimes exhibit a very high threshold for pain (APA, 2000), but those same individuals may be oversensitive to how their clothing touches their skin (Klinger et al., 2003). For instance, they may require all of the tags to be cut out of their shirts. Related to this, they sometimes have a fascination with certain sensory stimuli.

Case Example

Maria, a 4-year-old girl with autism, was preoccupied with strings. She typically carried a small string, which she twirled between her fingers. When she entered a room, she would immediately find the drawstring on the drapes or blinds and rub it repeatedly between her fingers. Notably, even in novel settings with new people or new toys, Maria was preoccupied with finding a string. In addition, she became easily overwhelmed by sounds and would cover her ears and rock back and forth if she perceived a sound to be too loud (even a far-off siren or a typical volume on the television or radio). She preferred heavy clothing and wanted to wear a jacket or coat at all times, even indoors and during hot summer months.

Because of their language delays and verbal communication deficits, individuals with an ASD have difficulty comprehending and responding to verbal explanations of information or expectations (Mesibov & Shea, 1996). They also have difficulty following behavior modeled by others, including social behaviors, because they lack imitation skills (Mesibov & Shea, 1996). They may not respond to social rewards and reinforcement (e.g., telling them that they have done a "good job") in the same manner as is typically observed and may be more motivated by their own stereotypic or repetitive behaviors and interests. Differences in language, cognitive functioning, movement, affect/mood, temperament, and other behaviors interrelate and contribute to the heterogeneity in the manifestation of symptoms observed in individuals with an ASD. Perhaps the most prominent source of variance among the ASDs is cognitive and intellectual functioning (Mesibov et al., 2004). Thus, two case examples, one for a low-functioning child with autism and one for a high-functioning child with autism, are described below to illustrate individual differences in how the characteristics and symptoms of an ASD may manifest.

Case History and Evaluation of a
Low-Functioning Child With Autism

Jane is a 4-year-old girl diagnosed with autism. Jane was born prematurely at 26 weeks gestation, weighing less than 2 pounds at birth. She had poor lung development and breathing problems at birth and was hospitalized for about 10 weeks due to complications from her prematurity. Jane's motor development was significantly delayed. She sat alone at 9 months, crawled at 14 months, and she did not walk until 22 months of age. Jane is not yet toilet trained. In the area of language development, Jane said her first words around 24 months of age. However, her speech mostly consists of echolalia (i.e., repeating words that her mother says with her mother's intonation). According to her mother, Jane will repeat words such as "cheese," "milk," and "cup," and she has recently begun repeating short phrases, such as "close the door" and "lock it." However, she engages in very little spontaneous communication.

Given that Jane's speech mainly consists of echoed words and phrases, she does not yet engage in "social babble" or reciprocal conversations with others. Jane does not point to request something, and if she tries to get her mother's attention, she usually throws a temper tantrum and her mother has to guess what she wants. Jane does not use gestures to communicate or indicate when she needs help. Jane often does not respond when her name is called. On the occasions when she does respond, she usually looks up, smiles, and then goes back to what she had been doing. Her mother reported that Jane understands fewer than 50 words.

Jane demonstrates a limited number of facial expressions. Her mother reported that she rarely looks sad and, rather, she usually looks confused when she is sad or in pain. Jane sometimes smiles, but it typically is when she is around someone with whom she is very familiar. She does not spontaneously share her interests with others. Additionally, Jane does not seem to pay attention to the feelings of others or attempt to comfort others. However, Jane does enjoy some social interaction games, such as peek-aboo and pat-a-cake. Jane has poor eye contact, and she usually looks at others out of the corner of her eye. She does not initiate interactions with other children and typically ignores them. Jane usually does not want to be approached by others, unless it is her siblings or parents. She becomes very upset if another child touches her or if he or she takes away one of her toys. Jane often prefers to play alone, instead of interacting with others. She does not yet engage in pretend or symbolic play, either alone or with others. Jane enjoys playing in mirrors, running up and down the hall at home, and exploring things. Although her mother often leaves toys out for her, Jane prefers to put keys in the socket, play with blinds and cords, and to push and pull a wagon. Jane often will inspect objects by smelling, sniffing, and staring at them out of the corner of her eye. She also enjoys sitting on her toys and rocking back and forth. Jane's mother reported that Jane walks on her toes, and she gets upset when told to stop.

During an assessment session, Jane was active, and it often was difficult to gain her attention to focus on the various tasks. For example, Jane did not respond to her name, despite having her mother and the examiner call her name several times. Although she appeared to enjoy some of the activities, such as watching bubbles and seeing the examiner blow up a balloon and then let it go, Jane rarely shared her enjoyment with her mother or the examiners. However, she tried to engage the examiner in an activity by using the bubble blower to put air on the examiner's face. Additionally, when asked to imitate the examiner when using a toy plane, Jane looked at her mother and the examiner, seemingly asking what she should do. Several times, it was difficult to get Jane to move from one activity to another. For example, she became very attached to the bubble blower, and she would put it up to her ear and turn in on repeatedly. Jane became very upset when the examiner tried to take this toy away to move on to other activities.

Jane engaged in a limited amount of language during the evaluation, saying a few one- or two-word phrases. When she did talk, she typically engaged in delayed echolalia. For example, when she tried to get inside a toy box that was in the testing room, Jane said, "Stand up." Her mother reported that she usually tells Jane to "stand up" in the bathtub, which was similar in size to the box. Jane also said a few short phrases to indicate what she wanted. Jane did not engage in reciprocal communication during the play session. She only spoke to the examiners a few times when she needed something from them. For example, when asked whether she wanted a cookie or a cracker for the snack, Jane initially reached for the crackers and tried to open the box on her own. She later said, "I wanna cracker" to the examiner to get more snack. Jane did not engage in pretend or imaginative play during the evaluation. Although she seemed interested in objects for a pretend birthday party for a doll, Jane did not appear to understand the concept of pretend play, and she did not respond to the examiner's requests to sing or blow out candles. With the exception of trying to blow air on the examiner with the bubble blower, Jane did not try to involve the examiner in her play.

Jane was very active during a cognitive testing session on another day. She was interested in putting her head near the air conditioning vent so that she could feel the air, and she enjoyed looking at herself in the mirror. Jane echoed several words from the instructions and the questions asked of her. For example, when asked to point to pictures, Jane repeated, "What's this?" after the examiner. Jane did engage in some pretend play, by pretending to stir food in a cup and eating it and by pretending that a circular puzzle piece was a cookie. Jane also had some difficulty during transitions. For example, she became very upset when blocks and pegs were taken away from her. However, she was able to calm down quickly. The cognitive evaluation, as well as an adaptive behavior interview with Jane's mother, indicated that her functioning is below the first percentile, indicative of comorbid mental retardation.

Case History and Evaluation of a High-Functioning Child With Autism

James is a 10-year-old boy with autism. James was born following an uncomplicated pregnancy and delivery. James has no known medical conditions and has never taken medication for behavioral or emotional problems. He met his early developmental milestones within normal limits. For example, he sat alone by 9 months, walked around the time of his first birthday, and was toilet trained by age 2.

In contrast, James demonstrated somewhat delayed language development. He said his first words around 1 ½ years and spoke in only a few short phrases at age 3. His language was very limited with a small vocabulary and few sentence constructions until age 4, and at this time he usually repeated words or phrases said by others. Before James developed meaningful speech, others usually had to initiate an interaction in order to determine when he needed something. For example, his mother would present him with options to drink, and he would indicate a preference by making a sound and pointing. He occasionally led her to the refrigerator saying "wa" when he wanted something to drink. Much of his early speech until around age 4 was echolalic. James began speech therapy when he started elementary school, and his ability to produce meaningful sentences improved greatly during his second-grade year. He currently has a large vocabulary and produces a range of grammatical structures. Still, his sentences consist of 4 to 5 words and are limited in quality or variety. James still exhibits some echolalia by repeating the last word of a phrase he just heard and calls his mother by her first name because that is what he hears others call her. James also has had difficulty enunciating words to the point that peers and strangers cannot understand what he says. This has improved somewhat as a result of speech therapy, but still contributes to his communication problems.

James currently joins in the conversations of others when he is interested in the topic; however, he does not maintain conversations very well. James does not seem to understand or use pronouns such as "she," "he," and "you" correctly, but he can use "I" to describe himself when appropriate. He uses a variety of gestures such as pointing to express interest and covering his mouth when he notices his siblings doing something wrong, and he used gestures to communicate before his speech improved. When James was younger, his mother suspected that he might be deaf because he would not respond to her. His teachers had similar concerns, and multiple hearing tests were conducted but results were negative. Although he responds more often now that he is older, his comprehension of language is very limited. He takes things literally and does not understand multiple names for a single object. James seems to comprehend language best when it occurs in the context of a familiar routine.

James seems to "tune others out" at times, and he does not maintain eye contact when talking to others. His interactions with others seem to interrupt him from play activities he prefers, and he seems disinterested or even frustrated by such interactions. When James was younger, he did not show interest or direct his mother's attention to things unless he saw something he was particularly interested in at that time, such as flashlights or pencil sharpeners. James now enjoys sharing objects of his interest with others, but he still has to be reminded to share food or toys. James currently shows a wide range of facial expressions but occasionally has inappropriate responses to some situations. For example, he laughs at his siblings or at peers when they are hurt, although he will stop if he realizes the situation is serious. Furthermore, even when James desires to interact with others, he seems to have difficulty understanding social nuances (e.g., never seems to understand sarcasm).

James enjoys many activities such as playing outside, watching movies, and playing with cars, specifically Hot Wheels™. When playing, James often imitates scenes from movies with his toys, but he participates in more creative pretend play, such as sword fighting and playing "school" with his siblings. James is somewhat timid about group games with other children and does not seem to understand the rules all of the time. James talks about friends he plays with at school, and he has a few close friends. James recently did not want a haircut because his friend had not had one. Still, he does not have a best friend with whom he has contact with outside of school.

James appears to have had several preoccupations with different objects over time. For example, when he was younger he really liked garage doors and wanted to open them repeatedly. He also liked pencil sharpeners and was given one as a gift. When James was told he could not open a garage door or play with a pencil sharpener, he would tantrum or become very upset. Currently, James talks a lot about fire alarms and likes to look at them and pull them when possible. James understands that he cannot do this, but he still gets upset and whines when told he cannot play with something he is interested in. James does get very upset and angry when his playtime with Hot Wheels™, his most preferred interest, is interrupted. He rarely plays with these cars appropriately and instead lines them up in a certain way every time and looks at the arrangement from different angles. He recently became angry and raised his voice when his mother accidentally bumped into the table where the cars were arranged. His play with Hot Wheels™ usually is limited in this way, but he occasionally races with his cars. James does not appear to have any other compulsions or rituals, and his response to changes in routine has improved over time. Although James used to repetitively rock in a chair, he currently displays no repetitive motor mannerisms. He occasionally smells objects before playing with them, but this does not occur routinely.

During an assessment session, James was motivated and cooperative and required little prompting from the examiner to complete the tasks. James seemed to enjoy the play session and was eager to please when attempting each task. James paid close attention to the examiner and made frequent eye contact while smiling. While attempting tasks, he sometimes talked to himself about what he was doing. James participated in joint pretend play with the examiner with some prompting, and he described what each toy was doing in his stories. He shared several of the activities with his mother, who was observing the session, and often looked back and forth to the examiner for assurance during the tasks. James asked the examiner a few questions about the tasks, and he asked her to repeat directions for one activity. Although somewhat limited in range, he used gestures during the play session, such as hand movements when telling a story. When presented with a puzzle, James was observed picking the pieces up and sniffing them before attempting the task.

When James was required to tell a story or describe an activity, he had considerable difficulty expressing his thoughts and ideas in complete, coherent sentences. He was skilled at providing some minor details, but could not elaborate when asked. For example, when talking about a pet frog, James explained that he caught it at his grandmother's house and took it home and fed it, but could not tell much more about the frog or what had happened to it. He also did not exhibit insight into social relationships. For example, when asked to describe friends, James said, "They do their work and they line up to go to the playground," which seemed to describe schoolmates instead. When asked to describe emotions, such as scared or angry, James could give examples or demonstrations of what the emotion looked like, but could not describe the concepts thoroughly. For example, he described scared as wanting to be by his mother. He provided a good portrayal of being angry by clenching his fists and using an angry tone of voice, but could not verbally describe the emotion. At times, it seemed like James's answers were limited by his ability to express his ideas, as evidenced by his apparent motivation and attempts to do so. Often James would change the topic when asked about difficult subjects such as getting along with peers and experiencing teasing.

During the cognitive testing session on another day, James was attentive to instructions and seemed motivated to do well and eager to please. He conversed spontaneously with the examiner, offering stories and asking questions throughout testing. James looked back and forth between test materials and the examiner and made frequent eye contact. At times, his language was inarticulate, as a result of stuttering and sound substitutions. It was observed that his language was more clear and understandable when he conversed spontaneously than when he answered test questions. James smiled throughout the session and used appropriate volume and tone of voice. James did not seem aware when he made mistakes, and experienced particular difficulty with arithmetic word problems. However, when he was allowed to complete these problems using numbers taken from the word problems, he was able to perform the required addition and subtraction operations correctly. James sometimes repeated aloud words presented by the examiner. On some verbal items, James would answer only portions of the question, such as defining only one word instead of the entire concept. On a test where he was asked to define words, James answered with an interesting pattern on every item administered. For example, he would say the first letter of the word and the definition, such as "*c* means you tell time" for *clock*. James responded to praise by smiling and asked for help on some difficult items. On one subtest, he repeatedly said, "How about this?" each time he finished with an item.

His test results showed that his intellectual functioning was generally within the average range, with some personal strengths and weaknesses. His academic achievement was average, with the exception of math, which was well below average. This is consistent with his everyday performance in school, where James has an Individualized Education Program (IEP) to address his academic, behavioral, and social needs. He often requires individual assistance in the regular classroom to maximize success. According to his school records, he is performing at grade level in reading and writing but is 2 years below grade level in math.

Conclusion

The symptoms, characteristics, and associated features of the autism spectrum disorders are quite heterogeneous. As such, there is no single case that exemplifies ASDs. Indeed, Mesibov and colleagues (2004) stated that "autism is the composite of the deficits, not any one characteristic" (p. 20). Understanding the characteristics associated with ASDs as potential sources for differences, both among individuals with an ASD and between those with and without these disorders, is an important first step in better assessment, diagnosis, and treatment of this complex set of disorders. Fortunately, the literature base regarding autism and related disorders has grown exponentially in recent years through the expansion and integration of empirical findings from genetic, cognitive neuroscience, and clinical studies. Such advances will continue to augment our understanding of the disorder so that better care may be provided.

Web Sites

American Academy of Pediatrics
http://www.aap.org/healthtopics/Autism.cfm

American Psychological Association
http://www.apa.org/topics/topicautism.html

Autism Research Institute
http://www.autism.com

Autism Society of America
http://www.autism-society.org/site/PageServer

Autism Speaks
http://www.autismspeaks.org

AutismAsperger.net
http://www.autismasperger.net

Centers for Disease Control and Prevention
http://www.cdc.gov/ncbddd/autism/overview.htm

Doug Flutie, Jr. Foundation for Autism
http://www.dougflutiejrfoundation.org

National Autism Association
http://www.nationalautismassociation.org

**National Institute of Child Health
and Human Development**
http://www.nichd.nih.gov/autism

National Institute of Mental Health
http://www.nimh.nih.gov

Organization for Autism Research
http://www.researchautism.org

UC Davis M.I.N.D. Institute—Autism Phenome Project
http://www.ucdmc.ucdavis.edu/MINDInstitute

Books

Boutot, E. A., & Tincani, M. (Eds.). (2009). *Autism encyclopedia: The complete guide to autism spectrum disorders*. Waco, TX: Prufrock Press.

Chez, M. G. (2008). *Autism and its medical management: A guide for parents and professionals*. Philadelphia: Jessica Kingsley.

Dodd, S. M. (2004). *Understanding autism*. New York: Elsevier.

Freeman, S., & Dake, L. (1997). *Teach me language: A language manual for children with autism, Asperger's syndrome and related developmental disorders*. Langley, BC: SKF Books.

Frith, U. (1992). *Autism and Asperger syndrome*. New York: Cambridge University Press.

Gallagher, P., Powell, T. H., & Rhodes, C. (2006). *Brothers & sisters: A special part of exceptional families.* Baltimore: Paul H. Brookes.

Grandin, T. (2006). *Thinking in pictures: My life with autism* (Expanded ed.). New York: Vintage Books.

Hamilton, L. M. (2000). *Facing autism: Giving parents reasons for hope and guidance for help.* Colorado Springs, CO: WaterBrook Press.

Hodgdon, L. A. (1999). *Visual strategies for improving communication: Practical supports for school & home.* Troy, MI: Quirk Roberts.

Hollander, E., & Anagnostou, E. (Eds.). (2007). *Clinical manual for the treatment of autism.* Washington, DC: American Psychiatric Publishing.

Janzen, J. (2003). *Understanding the nature of autism: A guide to the autism spectrum disorders.* San Antonio, TX: Harcourt Assessment.

Janzen, J. (2009). *Autism handbook for parents: Facts and strategies for parenting success.* Waco, TX: Prufrock Press.

Keating-Velasco, J. L. (2007). *A is for autism, F is for friend: A kid's book on making friends with a child who has autism.* Shawnee Mission, KS: Autism Asperger Publishing.

Koegel, L. K., & LaZebnik, C. (2005). *Overcoming autism: Finding the answers, strategies, and hope that can transform a child's life.* New York: Penguin.

Koegel, R. L., & Koegel, L. K. (Eds.). (1995). *Teaching children with autism: Strategies for initiating positive interactions and improving learning opportunities.* Baltimore: Paul H. Brookes.

Lathe, R. (2006). *Autism, brain, and environment.* Philadelphia: Jessica Kingsley.

Leaf, R., & McEachin, J. (Eds.). (1999). *A work in progress: Behavior management strategies and a curriculum for intensive behavioral treatment of autism.* New York: DRL Books.

LeComer, L. (2006). *A parent's guide to developmental delays: Recognizing and coping with missed milestones in speech, movement, learning, and other areas.* New York: Perigee.

Maurice, C. (1994). *Let me hear your voice: A family's triumph over autism.* New York: Ballantine.

Maurice, C. (Ed.), & Green, G., & Luce, S. C. (Co-Eds.). (1996). *Behavioral intervention for young children with autism: A manual for parents and professionals.* Austin, TX: Pro-Ed.

McClannahan, L. E., & Krantz, P. J. (1999). *Activity schedules for children with autism: Teaching independent behavior.* Bethesda, MD: Woodbine House.

McClannahan, L. E., & Krantz, P. J. (2005). *Teaching conversation to children with autism: Scripts and script fading.* Bethesda, MD: Woodbine House.

Moldin, S. O., & Rubenstein, J. L. R. (2006). *Understanding autism: From basic neuroscience to treatment.* Boca Raton, FL: CRC/Taylor & Frances.

Moyes, R. A. (2001). *Incorporating social goals in the classroom: A guide for teachers and parents of children with high-functioning autism and Asperger's syndrome.* Philadelphia: Jessica Kingsley.

Neisworth, J. T., & Wolfe, P. S. (Eds.). (2005). *The autism encyclopedia.* Baltimore: Paul H. Brookes.

Ozonoff, S., Dawson, G., & McPartland, J. (2002). *A parent's guide to Asperger syndrome and high-functioning autism: How to meet the challenges and help your child thrive.* New York: Guilford.

Ozonoff, S., Rogers, S. J., & Hendren, R. L. (2003). *Autism spectrum disorders: A research review for practitioners.* Washington, DC: American Psychiatric Publishing.

Peek, F., & Hanson, L. L. (2007). *The life and message of the real rain man: The journey of a mega-savant.* Port Chester, NY: Dude Publishing.

Powers, M. D. (Ed.). (2000). *Children with autism: A parent's guide.* Bethesda, MD: Woodbine House.

Schopler, E. (Ed.). (1995). *Parent survival manual: A guide to crisis resolution in autism and related developmental disorders.* New York: Plenum Press.

Seroussi, K. (2002). *Unraveling the mystery of autism and pervasive developmental disorder: A mother's story of research & recovery.* New York: Broadway Books.

Shore, S. (2003). *Beyond the wall: Personal experiences with autism and Asperger's syndrome* (2nd ed.). Shawnee Mission, KS: Autism Asperger Publishing.

Sicile-Kira, C. (2004). *Autism spectrum disorders: The complete guide to understanding autism, Asperger's syndrome, pervasive developmental disorder, and other ASDs.* New York: Perigree.

Sicile-Kira, C. (2006). *Adolescents on the autism spectrum: A parent's guide to the cognitive, social, physical, and transition needs of teenagers with autism spectrum disorders.* New York: Perigee.

Siegel, B. (1998). *The world of the autistic child: Understanding and treating autistic spectrum disorders.* New York: Oxford University Press.

Spencer, V. G., & Simpson, C. G. (Eds.). (2009). *Teaching children with autism in the general classroom.* Waco, TX: Prufrock Press.

References

American Psychiatric Association. (2000). *Diagnostic and statistical manual of mental disorders* (4th ed., Text rev.). Washington, DC: Author.

Ashtari, M., Bregman, J., Nichols, S., McIlree, C., Spritzer, L., Adesman, A., et al. (2007, November). *Gray matter enlargement in children with high functioning autism and Asperger syndrome using a novel method of diffusion based morphometry.* Paper presented at the annual meeting of the Radiological Society of North America, Chicago.

Barnhill, G. P. (2001). Social attributions and depression in adolescents with Asperger syndrome. *Focus on Autism and Other Developmental Disabilities, 16,* 46–53.

Baron-Cohen, S., & Bolton, P. (1993). *Autism: The facts.* New York: Oxford University Press.

Bauminger, N., & Kasari, C. (2000). Loneliness and friendship in high-functioning children with autism. *Child Development, 71,* 447–456.

Courchesne, E., Townsend, J. P., Akshoomoff, N. A., Yeung-Courchesne, R., Press, G. A., Murakami, J. W., et al. (1994). A new finding: Impairment in shifting attention in autistic and cerebellar patients. In H. Broman & J. Grafman (Eds.), *Atypical cognitive deficits in developmental disorders: Implications for brain function* (pp. 101–137). Hillsdale, NJ: Lawrence Erlbaum.

Couturier, J. L., Speechley, K. N., Steele, M., Norman, R., Stringer, B., & Nicolson, R. (2005). Parental perception of sleep problems in children of normal intelligence with pervasive developmental disorders: Prevalence, severity, and pattern. *Journal of the American Academy of Child and Adolescent Psychiatry, 44,* 815–822.

Dominick, K. C., Davis, N. O., Lainhart, J., Tager-Flusberg, H., & Folstein, S. (2007). Atypical behaviors in children with autism and children with a history of language impairment. *Research in Developmental Disabilities, 28,* 145–162.

Flanagan, D. P., & Kaufman, A. S. (2004). *Essentials of WISC-IV assessment.* New York: Wiley & Sons.

Fombonne, E. (2003). Epidemiological surveys of autism and other pervasive developmental disorders: An update. *Journal of Autism and Developmental Disorders, 33,* 365–382.

Frith, U. (2000). Cognitive explanations of autism. In K. Lee (Ed.), *Childhood cognitive development: The essential readings* (pp. 324–337). Oxford, England: Blackwell.

Happé, F. (1999). Autism: Cognitive deficit or cognitive style? *Trends in Cognitive Sciences, 3,* 216–222.

Hill, E. L. (2008). Executive functioning in autism spectrum disorder: Where it fits in the causal model. In E. McGregor, M. Núñez, K. Cebula, & J.-C. Gómez (Eds.), *Autism: An integrated view from neurocognitive, clinical, and intervention research* (pp. 145–165). Malden, MA: Blackwell Publishing.

Hoffman, C. D., Sweeney, D. P., Gilliam, J. E., & Lopez-Wagner, M. C. (2006). Sleep problems in children with autism and in typically developing children. *Focus on Autism and Other Developmental Disabilities, 21,* 146–152.

Klinger, L. G., Dawson, G., & Renner, P. (2003). Autistic disorder. In E. Mash & R. Barkley (Eds.), *Child psychopathology* (2nd ed., pp. 409–454). New York: Guilford.

Klinger, L. G., & Renner, P. (2000). Performance-based measures in autism: Implications for diagnosis, early detection, and identification of cognitive profiles. *Journal of Clinical Child Psychology, 29,* 479–492.

Konstantareas, M. M., & Stewart, K. (2006). Affect regulation and temperament in children with autism spectrum disorder. *Journal of Autism and Developmental Disorders, 36,* 143–154.

Lord, C. (1995). Follow-up of two-year-olds referred for possible autism. *Journal of Child Psychology and Psychiatry, 36,* 1365–1382.

Malow, B. A., Marzec, M. L., McGrew, S. G., Wang, L., Henderson, L. M., & Stone, W. L. (2006). Characterizing sleep in children with autism spectrum disorders: A multidimensional approach. *Sleep: Journal of Sleep and Sleep Disorders Research, 29,* 1563–1571.

McEvoy, R. E., Rogers, S. J., & Pennington, B. F. (1993). Executive function and social communication deficits in young autistic children. *Journal of Child Psychology and Psychiatry and Allied Disciplines, 34,* 563–578.

Mesibov, G. B., Adams, L. W., & Klinger, L. G. (1997). *Autism: Understanding the disorder.* New York: Plenum Press.

Mesibov, G. B., & Shea, V. (1996). Full inclusion and students with autism. *Journal of Autism and Developmental Disorders, 26,* 337–346.

Mesibov, G. B., Shea, V., & Schopler, E. (2004). *The TEACCH approach to autism spectrum disorders.* New York: Springer Science.

National Institute of Mental Health. (2008). *Autism spectrum disorders (Pervasive developmental disorders).* Washington, DC: Author. (NIH Publication No. 08-5511)

Osterling, J. A., Dawson, G., & Munson, J. A. (2002). Early recognition of 1-year-old infants with autism spectrum disorder versus mental retardation. *Development and Psychopathology, 14,* 239–251.

Ozonoff, S., & Jensen, J. (1999). Brief report: Specific executive functions profiles in three neurodevelopmental disorders. *Journal of Autism and Developmental Disorders, 29,* 171–177.

Ozonoff, S., Young, G. S., Goldring, S., Greiss-Hess, L., Herrera, A. M., Steele, J., et al. (2008). Gross motor development, movement abnormalities, and early identification of autism. *Journal of Autism and Developmental Disorders, 38,* 644–656.

Paavonen, E. J., Vehkalahti, K., Vanhala, R., von Wendt, L., Nieminen-von Wendt, T., & Aronen, E. T. (2008). Sleep in children with Asperger syndrome. *Journal of Autism and Developmental Disorders, 38,* 41–51.

Pennington, B. F. (2002). *The development of psychopathology: Nature and nurture.* New York: Guilford.

Piazza, C. C., Fisher, W. W., & Kahng, S. W. (1996). Sleep patterns in children and young adults with mental retardation and severe behavior disorders. *Developmental Medicine & Child Neurology, 38,* 335–344.

Richdale, A. L. (1999). Sleep problems in autism: Prevalence, cause, and intervention. *Developmental Medicine & Child Neurology, 41,* 60–66.

Richdale, A. L., & Prior, M. R. (1995). The sleep/wake rhythm in children with autism. *European Child and Adolescent Psychiatry, 4,* 175–186.

Schreck, K. A., & Mulick, J. A. (2000). Parental report of sleep problems in children with autism. *Journal of Autism and Developmental Disorders, 30,* 127–135.

Schreck, K. A., Mulick, J. A., & Smith, A. F. (2004). Sleep problems as possible predictors of intensified symptoms of autism. *Research in Developmental Disabilities, 25,* 57–66.

Schreck, K. A., Williams, K., & Smith, A. F. (2004). A comparison of eating behaviors between children with and without autism. *Journal of Autism and Developmental Disorders, 34,* 433–438.

Tager-Flusberg, H. (1993). What language reveals about the understanding of minds in children with autism. In S. Baron-

Cohen, H. Tager-Flusberg, & D. Cohen (Eds.), *Understanding other minds: Perspectives from autism* (pp. 138–157). Oxford, England: Oxford University Press.

Teitelbaum, O., Benton, T., Shah, P., Prince, A., Kelly, J., & Teitelbaum, P. (2004). Eshkol-Wachman movement notation in diagnosis: The early detection of Asperger's syndrome. *Proceedings of The National Academy of Sciences of The United States of America, 101,* 11909–11914.

Teitelbaum, P., Teitelbaum, O., Nye, J., Fryman, J., & Maurer, R. (1998). Movement analysis in infancy may be useful for early diagnosis of autism. *Proceedings of the National Academy of Sciences of The United States of America, 95,* 13982–13987.

Volkmar, F. R., & Lord, C. (2007). Diagnosis and definition of autism and other pervasive developmental disorders. In F. R. Volkmar (Ed.), *Autism and pervasive developmental disorders* (2nd ed., pp. 1–31). New York: Cambridge University Press.

Tammy D. Barry, Ph.D., is a child clinical psychologist and an assistant professor in the Department of Psychology at The University of Southern Mississippi (USM). She obtained her M.A. and Ph.D. from The University of Alabama and completed her clinical internship at The University of Alabama at Birmingham School of Medicine's Department of Psychiatry and Behavioral Neurobiology. After internship, Dr. Barry worked as a postdoctoral research fellow and adjunct assistant professor in the Department of Psychology at The University of Alabama. During that time, she also provided services and supervision at The University of Alabama's Autism Spectrum Disorder Clinic. Dr. Barry served as a visiting assistant professor at University of Louisville and an assistant professor at Texas A&M University before joining the faculty at USM. Dr. Barry's current research interests focus on child externalizing behaviors (e.g., Attention Deficit/Hyperactivity Disorder, oppositional defiant disorder, conduct disorder, aggression), as well as autism spectrum disorders. Specifically, Dr. Barry is interested in exploring contextual and biological correlates, including moderators and mediators, of these disorders.

Printed in the United States
by Baker & Taylor Publisher Services

Printed in the United States
by Baker & Taylor Publisher Services